Peter Stryker

A Historical Discourse

Delivered at the last service held in the Reformed Protestant Dutch

Church, corner of Broome and Greene Streets, New York City, April 15,

1860

Peter Stryker

A Historical Discourse
Delivered at the last service held in the Reformed Protestant Dutch Church, corner of Broome and Greene Streets, New York City, April 15, 1860

ISBN/EAN: 9783337309381

Printed in Europe, USA, Canada, Australia, Japan

Cover: Foto ©ninafisch / pixelio.de

More available books at **www.hansebooks.com**

A

HISTORICAL DISCOURSE

DELIVERED AT

THE LAST SERVICE

HELD IN THE

Reformed Protestant Dutch Church,

CORNER OF BROOME AND GREENE STREETS,

NEW YORK CITY,

APRIL 15, 1860.

BY THE PASTOR,

REV. PETER STRYKER.

Published by Request of the Consistory.

NEW YORK:

BOARD OF PUBLICATION
OF THE
REFORMED PROTESTANT DUTCH CHURCH,

SYNOD'S ROOMS, 61 FRANKLIN ST.

1860.

Closing Services.

THE Sanctuary belonging to the REFORMED PROTESTANT DUTCH CHURCH on the corner of Broome and Greene streets having been sold, the last religious services were held in it on Sabbath, April 15, 1860.

In the morning, at 10½ o'clock, a large audience assembled to hear the oldest living pastor, Rev. SAMUEL A. VAN VRANKEN, D.D., Professor in the Theological Seminary at New Brunswick, N. J., who discoursed about the Cloud overshadowing the Tabernacle, from Exodus 40: 34–38.

At two o'clock, P. M., a number of friends followed the remains of Mr. Thomas F. Peeney, a worthy disciple of Jesus, to the house of God, and listened to some remarks of the pastor, founded upon 1 Thessalonians 4: 14. Only two weeks before, Mr. Peeney was in the Sanctuary, apparently in his usual health. In common with many of his fellow members, he was looking forward with great interest to the last Sabbath in the Broome Street Church. His body was present, but the soul released from mortality, we trust was in the heavenly temple.

At 3½ o'clock, P. M., a throng again assembled in the old tabernacle, to listen to one who was the longest settled pastor, Rev. GEORGE H. FISHER, D.D., who discoursed concerning God as seen in the Sanctuary, from Psalm 63: 2.

It is an interesting fact, that at this service three little children were presented by their parents, in covenant to God by baptism.

In the evening, at 7½ o'clock, the Church was crowded to its utmost capacity, when the present pastor, Rev. PETER STRYKER, preached a Discourse on the History of the Church, which, by general request, and under the authority and supervision of the Consistory, is now published.

Discourse.

"AND THOU SHALT REMEMBER ALL THE WAY WHICH THE LORD THY GOD LED THEE."—*Deuteronomy* 8: 12.

FOR forty years Moses led the children of Israel in their march through the wilderness. At length they stand on the brink of Jordan, and soon will cross the stream, and enter the land of promise. But their leader cannot accompany them. He must be contented with a view of the goodly country from the top of Nebo. And very few of those who left Egypt will go over Jordan. Nearly all the old patriarchs have fallen victims to their perverseness and cupidity. It is for their children to receive the promised inheritance.

1*

To these young Israelites Moses speaks with all the tenderness and solicitude of a father who is soon to close his eyes in death. Part of his farewell advice we have in the words of our text.

Beloved people, among whom I have labored in the Gospel for nearly four years—years to me of much happiness, I trust to you of some benefit—in view of the change now transpiring in our experience as a Church, I can find no words more appropriate from which to preach to you the final discourse in this place, than those which were addressed by the distinguished Hebrew to his loving and beloved followers.

Let us, then, in gathering up our church reminiscences, previous to our removal, consider the way God has led us, and how we are to remember it.

I. In considering *the way God has led us*, we are introduced to the whole history of this Church from its incipiency to the present time.

And here, at the outset, an interesting fact meets us. This Church, which has been large and influential, in which much of the wealth of New York has been congregated, and from which even in the period of its financial embarrassment, large sums of money have been contributed to benevolent purposes—this Church was started as a missionary enterprise.

A society was organized, January 9th, 1822, called "The Missionary Society of the Reformed Dutch Church." The first missionary in their employ was the REV. ROBERT MC LEAN; and the first enterprise they originated through him was that which in a very short time resulted in the formation of this Church.

There was then no church of our denomination between Franklin street and the village of Greenwich. The society, therefore, determined to locate their missionary near the corner of Canal street and Broadway, a part of our city then growing rapidly. But as no suitable room could be obtained in that immediate locality, in which to hold divine service, the junction of Howard and Elm streets was selected as the central point of missionary operations. A room was there obtained, in which Mr. Mc Lean preached every Sabbath morning and evening, and in which he lectured one night in each week. With the exception of some twelve weeks in the summer of 1822, when the yellow fever was very prevalent, these exercises were continued in that place for about a year and a half, the attendance being very respectable, and the words of the preacher regarded as impressive.

But the room and locality were not attractive; and as persons of means and influence were joining the enterprise, it was determined to build a church edifice on the corner of Broome and Greene streets. Accordingly three lots of ground were purchased of Mr. Stephen Van Courtland, who conveyed them by deed to Messrs. Cornelius Hyer, Timothy Hutton, William Shaw, James

Bogert, Jr., and Gerard Beekman. These gentlemen were chosen as the building committee, and held the property in trust until the Church was organized.

The corner stone was laid in June, 1823. A large company of the prominent clergymen and laymen of the Reformed Dutch Church in the city of New York assembled on that occasion at the residence of a prominent citizen in Spring street, and walked in procession to this site; and then, in the presence of a numerous concourse of people, the venerable Dr. John H. Livingston, laid the corner-stone of this building, in the name of the Father, the Son, and the Holy Ghost, and accompanied this solemn ceremony with a most earnest and eloquent address.

In the month of October following, service was commenced in the basement, and from that time onward the indefatigable Missionary preached three times each Sabbath, and lectured once in the week.

On February 8th, 1824, this building was dedicated to the worship and service of the Triune God. On the morning of that day, Rev. Dr. Milledollar preached from 2 Chronicles 6: 18: "But will God in very deed dwell with men on the earth? Behold heaven and the heaven of heavens cannot contain Thee: how much less this house which I have built!" In the afternoon of the same Sabbath, Rev. Dr. Mc Murray preached from Psalm 89: 15: "Blessed is the people that know the joyful sound! they shall walk, O Lord, in the light of thy countenance." In the evening, Rev. Dr. Mathews preached from Ezekiel 37: 11: "Then he said unto me, son of man, these bones are the whole house of Israel." All these services were largely attended, and the names of the preachers afford sufficient evidence that they were conducted with interest.

The first cost of this building was $13,000, which, added to the cost of the lots, amounted to $16,200. This, however, does not include the ex-

pense of building the galleries and the front por-
tico, additions which were made a few years subsequent. To meet the expense incurred, $9,000
was obtained by subscription, and $7,000 be-
came a church debt, which, in three or four years,
was paid off.

This Church was organized by a committee ap-
pointed by the Classis of New York, on the second
Wednesday in December, 1823, when Messrs.
Luke Hinchcliff, and Stephen Hasbrouck, M.D.,
were installed elders, and Messrs. John Butler and
James Smith, deacons. Subsequently James
Smith was chosen clerk, and Leonard W. Kip,
Esq., treasurer.

Concerning this latter gentleman we must be
permitted to say a word in this connection. I trust
my worthy friend will pardon the mention of his
name and deeds, but as it is a part of the history I
must speak of him. With all the ardor of early
manhood, and trusting in God, he consented to
undertake the duties and responsibilities of church

treasurer. Through all the embarrassments neces-
sarily attending a new enterprise, he continued
at his post, by his energy, prudence and liberality,
carrying the Church safely through all its early
financial difficulties.

In the year 1835, about eleven years after the
organization of the Broome Street Church, Mr. Kip
resigned his office as treasurer, that he might give
his labors to the Reformed Dutch Church in Ninth
street, which was then an infant organization, under the pastoral care of his brother, the Rev. Fran-
cis M. Kip. During this period the late William
Hardenbrook, Jr., acceptably filled the office thus
rendered vacant. In the year 1838, Mr. Kip return-
ed to this Church, and was again elected treasurer.
Since that time he has annually been chosen to the
office, and at considerable sacrifice and with com-
mendable fidelity has fulfilled its important duties.
It is a remarkable circumstance, that he who,
more than thirty-six years ago, at the organization of this Church, was elected its treasurer,

is acting in that capacity still, and has been during the interesting period, with the exception of about three years. The shades with thee, beloved friend, are stretching lengthily in the past; but thy form bends forward, and thy step is toward heaven: and though thy eye is dim, and earth fades from thy view, soon with new vision thou wilt see the King in glory, and take thy place in the upper sanctuary. In the name of the Church, which thou so well hast served, I greet thee here to-night, and fervently invoke choice blessings on thy head. (*See Note A.*)

But let us return to our early history. The Church, having been organized ecclesiastically, was regularly incorporated under the title of "The Minister, Elders and Deacons of the Reformed Protestant Dutch Church in Broome Street, in the City of New York," by deed or declaration to that effect duly executed and acknowledged by the said elders and deacons, (there being then no installed minister,) dated January 26th, 1824, and recorded in the Register's Office, January 27th.

In the month of April, in the same year, the Rev. ROBERT McLEAN, who had acted first as missionary and then as stated supply, was called to the pastorate, and in the month of May was installed by a committee appointed by the Classis of New York. From that time onward the new vine, planted by the divine Gardener, as we believe, and watered with the dews and showers of grace, flourished more and more.

In the month of July, 1825, the pastor met with a severe trial, which almost paralyzed his energies. Mrs. McLean, who was a most estimable pious woman, and devoted wife and mother, was suddenly removed by death. Her remains were deposited beneath the edifice, under the floor of the lecture room, on the east side, and there they still repose. A kind friend of the old pastor and his wife, and of the Church, has generously signified he would remove this sacred dust to his private vault. (*See Note B.*)

The Rev. Mr. McLean continued pastor until April, 1826, when, with the consent of the Consistory, he resigned his charge, and with his two infant children sailed for Europe. He was an Englishman by birth, and on his return to his native country he became pastor of a dissenting church in Liverpool, in which the lamented Rev. Mr. Spencer preceded him, and which for many years has been under the care of the Rev. Dr. Raffles. He died a little before the year 1850, his two children, one of whom had arrived to manhood, having deceased before him. It is stated that their death greatly depressed his spirits and hastened his own.

This is all we can glean concerning the history of the first pastor of this Church. All who knew him and were accustomed to hear him preach, testify that he was a man of more than ordinary talent, a sound theologian, a forcible reasoner, a pleasant speaker, a man of piety and power. And his short ministry here—in all only about four years, in two of which he acted as missionary and two as pastor—was greatly blessed. As a preacher he was popular. Many of the intelligent and wealthy, as well as the humble classes, flocked to hear him. From the minutes of General Synod, held in 1825, we learn that during the preceding ecclesiastical ye ar, there were received to the Church under his ministry thirty-five persons by certificate, and twenty-seven by confession of faith, in all sixty-two. This, certainly, for an infant Church, was a large number, and indicates that the pastor was faithful and successful. Had he remained, and been able to overcome his mental depression induced by affliction, doubtless this Church, under his able ministrations, would have flourished as it did under his successor.

And now that the first pastor is gone, where shall the new and as yet feeble Church look for another ? The name of Dr. Brodhead was suggested. But by the majority the thought of procuring the services of so distinguished a divine was deemed altogether visionary. The voice of a few hopeful ones, however, prevailed. An urgent and uuanimous call, immediately after the resignation of Mr. McLean, was forwarded by a committee to the Rev. JACOB BRODHEAD, D.D., pastor of the Crown Street Reformed Dutch Church, in Philadelphia, which soon met with a favorable response. In a letter dated April 7th, 1826, Dr. Brodhead writes : "According to my promise, I now inform you that I have determined, in the fear of the Lord, to accept the call from you and the Church which you represent. I need not say to you, what you must have supposed, that this determination is accompanied with the most painful apprehension of the result. That I come at a sacrifice is well known, but that I shall not regard if the Lord is pleased to use me as an humble instrument to promote His glory and the cause of the Redeemer among you. I cast myself entirely upon Him, even upon Jehovah Jesus, my Saviour, whose I am and whom I desire to serve."

That it was with reluctance the Church in Philadelphia relinquished the services of their pastor is evident from the resolutions they passed in accepting his resignation, in which occurs the following language: "This Consistory sincerely regret the determination of the Rev. Dr. Brodhead to accept the call presented him, especially since his labors in this Church have been evidently succeeded by the blessing of the Most High; and since, from his faithful and persevering devotedness to the glory of the great Head of the Church, and the welfare of this our Zion, his tender and affectionate regard for the spiritual interest of the flock of which the Holy Ghost hath made him overseer,— and that for his private deportment as well as his public ministrations—he has become very much endeared to the people of his charge."

Thus, at a sacrifice on his own part and also on the part of his former people, that holy man came to take charge of this Church. He came because he felt that God, in a peculiar manner, called him, and had a great work for him here to

perform. He conferred not with flesh and blood.
He came as Peter went to Cæsarea, without gain-
saying, as soon as he was sent for. And the se-
quel proves he did right. God blessed him, and
made him a blessing to the people.

Well known as a popular preacher and pastor,
Dr. Brodhead did not fall back upon his former
fame. From the beginning he threw his whole
soul into the holy work of the ministry. He
preached plain, practical, pungent discourses, and
his acceptable pulpit services were followed by
equally faithful and pleasing pastoral visiting. As
a consequence, the Church was soon thronged with
attentive hearers, and the membership rapidly in-
creased. In less than four months every pew and
sitting in this edifice was rented, and then a gallery was erected. Soon this also was crowded, and
then the upper gallery was built for the accommo-
dation of the Sabbath school children. At this
time the Church was filled to its utmost capacity,
and continued so during Dr. Brodhead's pastorate

of over eleven years. It was a common thing for people of wealth to apply for seats six months in advance, and some who could not be accommodated went away weeping.

With a proper regard to appearance as well as convenience, it appears that early in the year 1828 a project was initiated, and in the course of the season prosecuted and completed, by which the iron railing was put around the Church, the wooden steps superceded by stone, and the columns in front erected, all at a cost of about $3,000. (*See Note C.*)

But we turn with greater pleasure to the statistics, which evidence the spiritual prosperity and growth of this portion of Zion in those days. From the Church records it appears there were received to the communion, during Dr. Brodhead's pastorate of eleven years, four hundred and ninety-one members, of which number two hundred and eighteen were admitted on confession of faith, and two hundred and seventy-three by certificate from other churches. During the whole of this period there never was a communion season that passed without some additions. This shows conclusively that the Church was in a healthy condition.

By many people this has been and is yet known as "Dr. Brodhead's Church." And there is good reason for it. He found it an infant enterprise, small and feeble. He nursed it carefully as a mother does her babe. He fed it with pure milk, and as it was able to bear it with the strong meat of the Gospel. And every thing favored his labor here. The cream of New York society was gathering in this vicinity when he came from Philadelphia, and up to the time when he left this pastorate, the wealthy, the intelligent, the pious were living near. The changes which have since occurred, and which have so thoroughly discouraged some of his successors, did not commence until shortly before his departure. And with these favorable circumstances in Providence, and his own peculiar fitness for the field of labor, the Spirit of God was

2

with our departed father, and gave a holy tone to his entire ministry.

Great anxiety was felt and expressed when it was known that the pastor was anticipating a removal. And when, in a kind and tender letter, he announced to the Consistory the necessity for such action, and asked them to unite with him in requesting Classis to dissolve the pastoral connection, they demurred—they said plainly, *no*. Compelled, however, to reconsider this vote, in giving up their beloved teacher, they declare: "While they deeply regret that his health has become so impaired as to render a change of residence necessary and a separation from his congregation unavoidable, still they would rejoice and bless God that he has been permitted for so many years to break unto them and to the congregation under their care the bread of life. They believe and are assured that his ministry among them has been owned and blessed of the Lord in the ingathering of souls, and in upholding the weak of the flock.

They thank God that in his late affliction he has been enabled to enjoy the comforts of that Gospel with which he has so often cheered the people of his charge under the chastening hand of their heavenly Father."

These were no words of formality, no ointment to heal up old sores. They were the expression of true and loving hearts. They were the outgushing of souls grateful for the past, and sad on account of the experience of the present.

I cannot close this portion of our history without giving a concise sketch of the life of him who was once so prominent in this Christian community, so useful and beloved in this Church, and who has gone to his rest and reward. The following facts are derived from the address delivered by Dr. De Witt at his funeral.

The Rev. Dr. Jacob Brodhead was born at Marbletown, Ulster co., N. Y., on the 14th of May, 1782. Having graduated from Union College in

1801, he immediately commenced the study of divinity with Dr. Solomon Froeligh. Called to act the part of tutor in Union College, he continued his theological studies under the direction of his uncle, Dr. Theoderick Romeyn. In April, 1804, he was licensed by the Classis of Albany to preach the Gospel. Immediately after his licensure he received a call from the Reformed Dutch Church of Rhinebeck. After a pleasant ministry there of five years, in the year 1809 he resigned his charge to accept a call from the Collegiate Church in the city of New York, and here became the colleague of Rev. Drs. Livingston, Kuypers, Abeel and Schureman. After much solicitation and with careful consideration, Dr. Brodhead, in 1813, accepted a call to become pastor of the Crown Street Reformed Dutch Church in Philadelphia. In that connection he remained thirteen years, honored by his neighbors, beloved by his people. In the year 1826 he was induced to return to New York, and become the pastor of this Church. After laboring here eleven years, on account of ill health he removed to Saugerties, Ulster co., N. Y., in 1837, and entered upon the pastorate of the Reformed Dutch Church of Flatbush, adjacent. His health being restored, he was induced, after much urgent solicitation, in 1841, to become the minister of the Central Reformed Dutch Church of Brooklyn; in this position he remained until the year 1846, when he resigned the pastoral office. After this he preached much for vacant churches, and for his ministerial brethren. During the winter of 1854 and '55, the winter preceding his death, Dr. Brodhead preached in this pulpit (then vacant) once each Sabbath. In April, 1855, his health failing, he visited his daughter at Springfield, Mass., and there, in the arms of his beloved and honored son, J. Romeyn Brodhead, Esq., and of his affectionate daughter, Mrs. George M. Atwater, he gently breathed his last breath, June 6th, 1855, aged 73 years and 23 days. His precious remains were brought hither, and after appropriate and impressive exercises in the North Dutch Church, were entombed in the ministers'

vault attached to that building. The whole Church
mourned.   General Synod, then in annual session
at New Brunswick, N. J., passed resolutions of respect to his memory, and delegated a committee
of twelve to attend his funeral.   Devout men of
every persuasion followed him to his burial, and
the tidings of his death gave sorrow to many
Christians throughout the land.

The Rev. Dr. Bethune, in a commemorative
discourse, thus speaks of him : "Having dedicated himself to God in his fresh youth, he kept his
vow steadily unto the end.   So far from losing the
warmth of his love, it grew with his experience
and his knowledge of the Saviour.   This, doubtless was assisted by the strength of his constitution,
his ardent temperament and healthful disposition.
No one could look on his marked, pleasing features,
expressive of thought and feeling, his tall, manly
frame, and his easy, prompt movement, without
recognising a sound mind in a sound body.   Frank,
generous and kind, he appeared what he was.

When he gave you his hand, you knew that his heart came with it; and his smiles or tears were natural as a child's.

" It is no wonder, then, that, under the influence of religion, he was what he was. Firm, yet not impassible; consistent, yet not pragmatical; steadfast in faith and virtue, but free from exacting bigotry and petty scrupulosities; fearless in censure of vice and damning error, yet tolerant of human weakness; covetous of converse with the gravely wise and wisely good, yet affectionately considerate of the young and delighting to take little children up in his arms; open to approach, and winning in his advances; so mingling freely with all classes, but ever mindful of his allegiance to the kingdom which is not of this world, he proved not less in the common duties of daily life than in the fellowship of Christian solemnity, that his piety was a dominant principle, maintained by habitual communion with God, study of the Scriptures and contemplation of eternal things."

I have thus entered somewhat particularly into the character of the first two pastors as well as the history of the Church in their time. It was proper to do so, because these dear fathers in the ministry have gone from earth. They rest from their labors, and their works do follow them ; and moreover, under their pastorates, the Church was organised and established.

My other predecessors in this charge are still living, each one to speak for his Master as well as himself ; and if the history of the Church is not as replete with interesting incidents in their time as it has been before and since, it is because the river runs more quietly in its deep, broad channel than when, a little rill, it plunges in a noisy way down the mountain side and over its pebbly bed, or when near its mouth it wildly dashes over the rapids into the sea.

A fact is here worthy of notice. It has never been the policy of this Church to wait long after losing a pastor before endeavoring to secure another, and in this endeavor they uniformly have been successful. During a very little time has this pulpit been vacant. The eyes of the people have constantly seen their teachers, and their ears have ever heard a voice behind them saying, This is the way, walk ye in it. Scarcely had Mr. McLean resigned his call and embarked for Europe before Dr. Brodhead was standing in his place to announce the message of life. And so when the latter retired to the country to relax and strengthen his weary powers, at once his successor was chosen in the person of SAMUEL A. VAN VRANKEN, D.D., who for many years had been the popular pastor of the First Reformed Dutch Church of Freehold, N. J., and at that time was preaching with great acceptance in the Reformed Dutch Church of Poughkeepsie. We need not wonder that our excellent friend, then in the prime of life, at first declined to leave a village one of the most enterprising and pleasant in the country, and a Church which was and is still among the most intelligent and desirable in our connection. He positively declined. But Broome Street was per-

2*

severing.   The call was renewed.   The importance
of the field was mentioned, the unanimity of the
people urged, and at length the country yielded—
the city conquered.   In a letter to the Consistory
of this Church, dated December 6, 1837, but a few
weeks after Dr. Brodhead's dismission, Dr. Van
Vranken writes that he will come if he can get a
release from his present charge : and in December,
1837, he was installed as pastor of this Church by
the committee appointed for that purpose by the
Classis of New York.

After a faithful ministry of four years, during
which he endeared himself to many without as well
as within this congregation, Dr. Van Vranken was
in the autumn of 1841 elected by the General Synod to fill the chair of Didactic and Polemic Theology in the Theological Seminary at New Brunswick, rendered vacant by the resignation of Rev.
Dr. Milledollar.   In a minute of their proceedings,
dated October 25th, the Consistory say they "deeply regret the loss of the services of their beloved

pastor. Yet they feel gratified that he has been called to duties of higher and more extended usefulness. And being fully convinced that it is his duty to the Church at large to accept the responsible office conferred on him by Synod, they do agree to unite with him in application to Classis, according to his request, commending him to God, whose he is and whom he serves, and praying that the precious truths of the Gospel, which he has for four years past been permitted to proclaim in their midst, may be as good seed, which shall spring forth and bear a glorious harvest." In a subsequent minute we find a resolution to the effect that a delegation of six be appointed to attend the inauguration of the Rev. Dr. Van Vranken as Professor of Theology in the Seminary at New Brunswick, on the 14th day of December next.

For nearly twenty years has our worthy friend continued in this position, an honor and blessing to the Church of his fathers. Many of our present ministry have felt it a privilege to sit at his feet, as Paul did at the feet of Gamaliel, to receive from his warm heart and parental lips those lessons of wisdom which they in turn have been and still are giving to the Church and the world.

Beloved Instructor, may you long be spared to grace the holy office given you, to teach our young prophets, and through them to speak to millions more! And when the mandate comes to summon you to join the sainted Livingston, Milledollar, Cannon, Ludlow, and others who have passed away, may you, like them, gently fall asleep in the arms of Jesus, and awake to the enjoyment of everlasting life and glory!

In the good providence of God, the eyes of the Broome Street Church were now turned to the Rev. GEORGE H. FISHER, pastor of the Reformed Dutch Church, of Hudson, N. Y., and who, previous to this, was pastor, first, of the Reformed Dutch Church of North Branch, and then of the Reformed Dutch Church of Fishkill. It was no doubt a sad and difficult task to tear away from a beloved

Church to which, for six years, he had ministered, which was organised under his supervision, and from infancy had been nursed by him like a child, and amid which he had formed many pleasant associations. But the unanimity of the call and the prospect of enlarged usefulness induced our beloved brother to make the sacrifice. He came, and on February 13, 1842, was installed by a committee appointed by Classis, Rev. Prof. Van Vranken, by request, preaching the sermon, and Rev. Dr. Brodhead delivering the charge to the pastor and people.

For a longer time was Dr. Fisher settled here than any pastor before or after him. For a period of more than thirteen years—a long period in these days of ministerial mutation—he went in and out before this Church and congregation, breaking to them the bread of life. At many a sick bed did he stand to give comfort and encouragement, in many a desolate habitation did he enter, carrying the cheerful lamp of the Gospel. Not a few departing souls have breathed out with their latest breath rich blessings on their pastor's head, and many yet live, some here, more elsewhere, to praise God they were permitted here to enjoy the ministry of my beloved brother for so many years.

It is proper here to mention that in the year 1843, during the pastorate of Dr. Fisher, the interior of this building was considerably modified, adding much to its appearance and comfort. This pulpit was then built, the pews were cut down and surmounted with new mahogany tops and scrolls, and furnished with new upholstery. For these repairs and additions, an expense of about $3,300 was incurred.

In the month of December, 1854, Dr. Fisher received a call from the Reformed Dutch Church of Utica, which he deemed it proper to accept. In a letter, addressed to the Broome Street Consistory, he writes: "You are aware, the reasons inducing me to accede to a request to change my

field of labor, arise solely from the difficulties with
which the constant and increasing removals of the
people of the Church and congregation, from the
vicinity of our house of worship, have surrounded
us. And now, in connection with the importance
of the pastoral charge offered to me, and the
unanimity of voice with which I am happy to say
the people of that Church have spoken, they have
drawn me to the conclusion that it is my duty to
remove from New York to Utica." What could
this Consistory say or do? They loved their pastor. They knew the people loved him. But they
could not be selfish. Satisfied that his welfare
demanded it, with sorrowing hearts they consented that the tie which had so long bound them
to their minister should be sundered, and then,
having borne sincere testimony to his faithfulness
and love, they bade him and his beloved house-
hold farewell, and followed them with prayers
and tears to their new home. Five long years,
peculiar years to this Church, have elapsed since
that hour of sad separation; but doubtless there

are many here to-day, whose minds bound over
the intervening period as if it were only a point of
time; and, as they remember the sunny days of
the past, rejoice even now, when a dense and
gloomy cloud is lowering over the tabernacle, to
see their old pastor; old, I mean not in his years,
but in his relation to them; and their ears have
to-day listened with delight to the mellow tones of
his familiar voice. I know I but echo the feelings
of the flock, beloved brother in the ministry, and
predecessor in this charge, when I say, "God bless
you, spare your life to a good old age, continue
your usefulness even to the end, and then reünite
you to those loved ones of your family, and others
of this fold, who have gone before to glory!"

Discouraged by the loss of their pastor, there
was now a strong inclination manifested on the
part of the Consistory and congregation to change
the location of the Church. But God had determined this should not yet occur, and in his providence directed attention to a young and talented

brother, who for three years had been pastor of the Reformed Dutch Church of Geneva. The Rev. HENRY V. VOORHEES was called, and having accepted the invitation was installed pastor of this Church, by a committee appointed by Classis, in the month of May, 1855.

The ministry of our beloved brother seemed likely to prove a wonderful success. Possessing many elements of popularity, his fame soon spread abroad, and numbers crowded hither to hear him. But, alas! all hopes were soon cast to the ground. Assailed by disease, the preacher, after a few Sabbaths of service was prostrated, and a second trial was followed by a similar result. It being evident that the sick pastor needed perfect rest, by the advice of his physicians he resigned his call, December 20, 1855, less than three fourths of a year from the date of his installation. Convinced that it was their duty to him and the Church to do so, the Consistory reluctantly accepted the resignation, deploring the necessity which compelled them to this action, and invoking from the great Head of the Church, in behalf of their retiring pastor, restoration to health and prolonged usefulness in the Church.

For a year or more our brother was prevented by sickness from attending to the duties of his holy office. But it is a matter of joy to this people, and of congratulation to the whole Church, that he has been able for three years past to labor in the vineyard, having been called to and installed pastor of the Reformed Dutch Church of Bound Brook. May his bow long abide in strength, and like his Master may he increase in favor with God and man.

Subsequently a call was made upon the Rev. Alexander R. Thompson, of Staten Island, which, although twice presented, was twice declined.

In the month of April, 1826, a call was made upon the Rev. PETER STRYKER, then pastor of the Reformed Dutch Church of Rhinebeck, previously

of the Third Reformed Dutch Church of Raritan.
Having accepted the call, Mr. Stryker entered
upon his duties here the second Sabbath in May,
and on Sabbath evening, June 1st, was installed
pastor of this Church by the committee appointed
by Classis, his father, Rev. H. B. Stryker, by request, preaching the sermon, Rev. Dr. Vermilye
delivering the charge to the pastor, and Rev.
Jeremiah S. Lord the charge to the people. And
he who was then united to you in this most important and tender relation, rejoices, that after the
vicissitudes of nearly four years, he is still permitted to sustain toward you that relation, and to
greet you as his beloved people, his joy and
crown.

To speak of my own ministry is a delicate and
by no means enviable task. Yet I would be very
faulty as a chronicler did I not mention some facts
which constitute a part, and a very important part
too, of our history.

God has greatly favored us, dear flock. He who

came among you with much trembling and weakness, is to-day physically stronger than he was four years ago; and you who were then but few in number are now quite a multitude.

But notwithstanding all our increase in other particulars, it has for some time been evident we were greatly on the wane in our fiscal arrangements. That blackest of all clouds, a church debt, was brooding over us. We could not drive it away either by our prayers or efforts. Despite all our financiering it grew thicker and darker. With all due respect to our good old fathers, many of whom are now we hope in heaven, and to our beloved brethren who still hold the reins of government, we are compelled to say, in review of the past, this Church has been generous to a fault. It has provided for all but itself. Ever ready to contribute to causes of benevolence, in its palmy days, when the thing could have been prevented, it permitted a debt to be formed. And this creature, at first only a little thing, has grown to be a perfect monster, a very tyrant that stands over us with whip and scourge, and threatens to drive us to destruction.

The Collegiate Church very kindly gave us a thousand dollars a year for three years, their benefaction beginning in May, 1855, and ending in May, 1858. This was of great assistance. When our brethren felt compelled to withdraw this aid, the congregation, then very much enlarged in numbers and quickened in energy, were rallied, and nobly subscribed for the ensuing year the sum of $1,700. The year following, that which is now near its close, found the people still ready, but not so able. Last May many of our wealthy patrons moved away, and the subscription was reduced to $1,300. At no time was the amount subscribed by our people, or generously donated to us by our neighbors, adequate to meet the deficiency existing.

It became evident, a year or more ago, to those intrusted with the financial affairs of the Church, that this state of things could not last. It was ruinous. Nay, something must immediately be done. Not only was our debt like a rolling snow ball, increasing rapidly in size, but like a huge weight which one was trying to roll up hill, all the while threatening to come down upon the mover and crush him to powder. We needed help for the present emergency. It was earnestly solicited but came not. The only alternative was to move. (*See note D.*)

Just at this period of time, the LIVINGSTON RE-FORMED DUTCH CHURCH, worshiping in a hall on the corner of Thirty-third street and Eighth avenue, made overtures to us. They proposed in their weakness to merge into us, on condition that we would agree eventually to move up and build a Church in their vicinity. This proposition cost them a great sacrifice. It supposed the removal of their beloved pastor, Rev. F. N. ZABRISKIE, who had labored among them faithfully and with considerable success for three years—the loss of their name, the very best name, we think, in the Dutch

Church—the breaking up of their Church organization—the blotting out of one of the stars in our
ecclesiastical firmament—the frustration of long
and fondly-cherished hopes—the formation of new
and to them uncertain associations. I know they
had much to gain. But let it not be forgotten
those dear brethren had much also to lose. The
poor man's home is pleasant to him, be it ever so
homely, and it is not without a heart struggle that
he breaks from it, to find lodgment beneath a loftier
roof or in a statelier mansion.

But the proposition to coälesce supposed a sacrifice also on the part of the Broome Street Church,
a very great sacrifice, as we all felt then, and feel
perhaps more deeply now. At first, therefore, the
offer was declined. But the inability of this congregation to furnish the requisite means, even for present emergency, compelled the Consistory to reconsider this action. They in turn made overtures to
the Livingston Church, which were accepted, and
the proposed union was consummated. The Classis

of New York, to which both bodies belonged, approved the action ; the members of the Livingston Church were transferred to us, and since May, 1859, we have been one.

Very fortunately, we obtained the able services of the Rev. Professors CAMPBELL and WOODBRIDGE, of New Brunswick, to assist in preaching. These brethren, in company with the Rev. H. B. STRYKER, supplied the up-town congregation during the summer very acceptably.

Last autumn it became evident we could struggle with our dilapidated finances no longer. We must make arrangements for moving in the spring. The pastor accordingly, by request of the Consistory, and with the consent of the Professors, occupied the Chapel pulpit every Sabbath evening, and lectured there once during the week, while the Professors in turn have supplied the pulpit in Broome Street every Sabbath afternoon.

In the mean while, negotiations were pending

for the sale of this property. (*See Note E.*) This object was at length accomplished, and eligible building lots were also purchased in Thirty-fourth street. In the new location the work is progressing. The ground is nearly ready for the builders, and we are to-night, April 15th, 1860, holding service for the last time in our old and beloved Sanctuary.

I have thus rapidly sketched the history of this Church from its infancy to the present time, viewing each pastorate separately. Permit me to add a few facts in general review.

The statistics show that there have been, in the period under consideration, between thirty-six and thirty-seven years, 488 marriages solemnized by the pastors; 557 infants have been baptized, and 1,204 members have been admitted to this communion, of which number 688 have joined us by certificate from other Churches, and 516 on confession of their faith. At almost every com-

3

munion, since the organization of the Church,
some additions have been made. The grace of
God has thus descended upon us like the dew,
gently, constantly, refreshingly.

While many who have here given themselves
to the Lord have gone forth to other Churches in
this city and throughout our land, and as laymen
are exerting a hallowed influence for Christ, a few
here converted have devoted themselves to the
ministry of reconciliation. The Rev. WILLIAM R.
GORDON, D.D., now pastor at Schraalenburgh,
lately in the Seventh Avenue Church in this city;
Rev. ISAAC P. STRYKER, who went out as a missionary to Borneo, but died before he commenced
his labors for the conversion of the heathen; and
Rev. BENJAMIN C. LIPPINCOTT, pastor of the united
Churches of Hurley and North Marbleton, were
all the children of this Church. Here they em-
braced the Saviour, here espoused his cause, here
devoted themselves to the ministry, and here they
were supported while engaged in their prepara-

tory studies. Rev. HARVEY D. GANSE, pastor of
the Twenty-third Street Reformed Dutch Church,
in this city, was for many years a pupil in our
Sabbath school; and perhaps others have been
more or less intimately connected with us, who are
now occupying important places in the Master's
vineyard. Nor must I fail in this connection to
speak of LEONARD W. KIP, Jr., very dear to me as
my son in the Gospel, who is now completing his
studies in our Theological Seminary, and who,
having been accepted by our Board of Foreign
Missions, expects, in the course of the ensuing
year, to go forth as a missionary to the heathen.

The Sabbath school here has been a highly
cherished, carefully conducted, deeply interesting,
and there is every reason to believe most profita-
ble institution. Who that knew him, had seen his
smiling face, and heard his stirring voice, will forget the old superintendent WILLIAM WORAM, who
commenced this school as soon as the lecture room
was opened, and for eighteen years conducted it,

and, until his death, evinced a warm interest in
its welfare? Nor do we believe that the services
of his successors, Bauman Lowe, Louis J. Belloni,
John Woolsey, James V. Freeman, and A. C.
Stryker, nor of the other Christian men and
women who have filled other offices, will soon
fade from remembrance. And fresh and sweet as
the laurel to the heart of many a scholar, we are
sure will be the instructions of those faithful
teachers whose names cannot be mentioned now,
but whose witness is in heaven, whose record is on
high.

And if we may be permitted to exhibit a little
vanity, we will speak again of the *benevolence* of
. this Church. In very few portions of Zion has
the spirit of gospel liberality been more apparent
than here. All the worthy causes have in turn
received attention, and some have been largely
patronized. In the early period of its existence,
the Broome Street Church had an auxiliary to the
American Colonization Society. From a report

in the handwriting of the late Mr. Samuel Kip, secretary, it appears that in the year 1833 there was contributed by this Church to that society the sum of $300. The children have been trained to deeds of benevolence, and for many years have collected in their missionary society in the Sabbath school, and contributed to our Board of Domestic Missions, the sum of $300 a year toward the support of the Mission of the Thousand Isles in the St. Lawrence river. I think the Lord must love this people. He says he loves the cheerful giver, and such unquestionably are some of these. Even the last year, when straining every nerve to support this sinking enterprise, the Broome Street Reformed Dutch Church has contributed to benevolent purposes nearly $3,000. Nor do we believe this has been given from vain show. Much of it has quietly, unostentatiously been bestowed by those in humble circumstances. Love for souls and a desire for God's glory has engendered self-denial. And this self-denial has with many been the result of fixed principle, and systematic ar-

rangement, not the offspring of excited emotion.
(*See Note F.*)

II. Such is the way the Lord has led us. Now
let us secondly and briefly consider *How we
should remember it.*

1. We cannot now think of it without a feeling
of *sadness.* Changes always denote imperfection;
they remind us of sin, the cause of all our woe.
Those which transpire regularly, as the alternation
of day and night, of winter and summer, and the
succession of childhood, youth, manhood and old
age, bring to the thoughtful mind at times a tinge
of melancholy. Every thing around us is mutable; ever mutable; even the countenances, forms,
voices, actions, perhaps affections of those we most
dearly love.

> "Ah, me! what is there in earth's various range
> Which time and absence may not sadly change?"

Like the fleecy cloud, the birds in autumn time,
the flowing stream, the dew-drop of the morning,

so all things else are passing away. This world is
a vast moving panorama, and as the scene glides
onward, we, too, move, and all are hastening to
the grave of the future—the oblivion of the past,
except that which is immortal.

But we are now the victims of peculiar change.
Remorseless time has made especial havoc in
our midst. Who can but sigh as he beholds the
fairest portions of our city, once inhabited by the
good and great, now abandoned to filthy lucre,
natural pollution, and moral degradation? But
most of all to be deprecated is the removal of our
churches. We cannot but regard this as vandal-
ism, necessary though it is. Look at these hallowed walls—strong as when they were first rear-
ed; at this pleasant sanctuary, so commodious and
symmetrical; at these pews, in which so many
have worshiped God, and in which, up to the
present time, despite the changes, a goodly throng
have regularly assembled. Look at this pulpit,
from which, for many years, the Word of God has

been proclaimed, and then ask, "Why must this all come to desolation?" But why institute the inquiry? It is quite useless. The fact itself is perceptible. We follow down the stream of history for the last score of years, and we discern changes—changes. We see the moth insidiously but surely accomplishing destruction. Like the traveler, we sit down amid the holy ruins, and sigh at the ravages of time. We weep for the days of old. For ourselves we weep. How can we leave these holy courts, where so often we have held delightful converse with each other and the Lord? Like the Hebrew bard in Babylon, we exclaim, in the bitterness of our souls, "How can we sing the Lord's song in a strange land?" And more profusely still our tears flow forth for those who live in sin around this house of God. Soon these sacred walls will no longer in mute but mighty eloquence remonstrate against iniquity; and this minister will no longer appear in times of funereal sorrow or connubial bliss to speak a word in this vicinity for Jesus.

O ! we cannot but feel sad. Nature will weep, and grace stands by and bids the gushing fountain flow. Happy for us, my hearers, if in this season of sorrow we have, in the retrospection of the past, no personal errors to mourn; no derelictions to lament; if, while our souls cleave unto the dust, each can lay his hand upon his heart, and say, "To the utmost of my power I have done my duty to God and my fellow men, for the welfare of this Church, and the reformation of the surrounding Sodom."

2. But, beloved people, we should also remember the way which God has led us with *gratitude*. While we sorrow, let us not forget the blessings of the past, and those which now are mingled with adversity. In reviewing the days and years gone by, do we not see much to fill our hearts with joy, and to call forth now and ever the praises of our lips? Think how kindly God has led you, and your fathers and mothers, who now sleep in the dust of the earth! Think of the great and nu-

3*

merous privileges here enjoyed, the words of in-
struction that have fallen from earnest lips, the
consolation you have received in times of be-
reavement, the pleasant intercourse with Christian friends, the sweet music to which you have
listened and in which you have joined! Think
of the devout supplications offered up here in your
behalf, the gentle breathings of the Holy Ghost
wooing your souls to repentance and faith, the
angels bending from heaven to catch your first
penitential sigh, and carry it with joy to heaven!
And think, too, of your wishes here accomplished;
of children, parents, partners, friends, who, in an-
swer to your fervent prayers here offered, have
been raised from the borders of the grave, or have
bowed in contrition at the Cross, and here in full
faith have taken your Saviour to be theirs! Think
of the good seed here sown, which yet may spring
from the heart, and bear fruit to the glory of God!
Think of the Word which has here been treasured
up and carried forth to every portion of our land
by earnest, self-denying Christians, and which,

after this temple is demolished, may be conveyed
to China, India or the isles of the sea! Think of
the prayers and alms which have come up as a
memorial before God, and which will be influential
while the world lasts. O, friends, this Church has
been no failure. From beginning to end it has
been a success. Most signally has God blessed it.
And to Him be all the glory! The departed Mc
Lean and Brodhead cry ever before the throne,
"To Him be all the glory"! These pastors on
earth cry out, "To Him be all the glory"! The
whole Church, past, present and to come, in earth
and heaven, here and every where, unite in the
shout, "To Him be all the glory"! "Blessing
and honor, and glory and power, be unto Him
that sitteth upon the throne, and unto the Lamb
for ever"!

Pastors have reason to thank God that they have
here been permitted to preach to an intelligent,
attentive, loving, working, benevolent people.
And the people may thank God (I speak now of

my predecessors, not myself) that they have been
favored with the ministry of men, all but one train-
ed up in our Reformed Dutch Church, all attached to our institutions, all evangelical in their
teachings, all men of piety, prudence, prayer,
and fearless in their advocacy of truth. Blessed
be God, the history of this Church is no mean
record. It will bear inspection. This we say not
in vain boast, but in devout gratitude. For it is
all of God.

3. We should also remember the way God has
led us with *hope*.

This hope, brethren, is a great support. A
sweet writer has said :

> "She lights our gloom—she soothes our care—
>   She bids our fears depart;
> Transmutes to gems each grief-fraught tear,
>   And binds the broken heart.
>
> She glances o'er us from above,
>   The brightest star that 's given,
> And guides us still, through faith and love,.
>   To endless peace in Heaven."

The youthful bride, going forth from the parental roof, weeps at the breaking up of old associations, but her heart is buoyant with expectation of sweeter joys to spring from the new relation formed. The emigrant, forced by stern necessity to leave the home of his childhood, the land of his birth, sheds many bitter tears, but as he turns his eye across the deep blue sea to the far-off country where he understands that peace and plenty, law and liberty, are dominant, his drooping spirits are aroused, and hope exultant springs up in his breast.

Shall it not be so with us as a Church? Some I know must leave us, and to such I feel that I am now preaching my farewell discourse as a pastor. But, beloved, though we part, we hope to meet again. Review the past. Remember the way God has led us. And will he not still direct your footsteps? He will if you trust in Him as your Guide. Perhaps in more pleasant pasture fields, and beside more cooling streams, he will conduct

you in life's pilgrimage. But let the eye of hope
look farther. Beyond these earthly scenes, when
the scroll of time is rolled together and sealed;
when earth, with its changes, has forever faded
from our vision, then, dear flock, from whom we
part to-night, then we shall meet again.

"O Heaven is where no secret dread
  May haunt love's meeting hour;
Where, from the past, no gloom is shed
  O'er the heart's chosen bower;
Where every severed wreath is bound—
  Where none have heard the knell
That smites the heart with that deep sound—
  Farewell, beloved, farewell!"

But will we *all* meet there? Would we could
with assurance say : *Yes, all.* But you know full
well that none but they who trust in Jesus can
gain entrance there. Let me again ask you, some
of you perhaps for the last time, say, will you go
with us to Mount Zion? How my heart yearns
over you! With these poor lips I have often told
you of Jesus. Bear me witness that, with all my

infirmities I have never withheld from you the plain
Gospel. In the name of Him I serve I have warn-
ed, expostulated, entreated. And now again I
invite you who are yet impenitent to meet us in
glory. I trust you will not turn from the divine
Son of God, though you may from his unworthy
servant. In the calm evening hour of the Sabbath
day, and amid these solemn closing scenes, I pray
God that he will now impress every mind, and
lead us all to Jesus' cross, and from the cross onward and upward to the crown in heaven!

But hope inspires us with reference to the way
yet before us, as well as the promised land beyond.
This Church does not cease its existence. It will
live, although elsewhere. And its prosperity in
the past is, we trust, a harbinger of still greater
and more lasting usefulness in the future. Convinced that we have done our duty, that God in
his providence is leading us, we go forward, not
dispirited, but hopeful. Many of this congregation have anticipated us in our removal. Year

after year they have gone up, and doubtless not a few will join us and our new friends in the new home.   Some go with us, others will follow. There is a tie that binds many to us which will not yet be severed.   We know there are those who have a life interest in this Church, who have too long been attached to it, too faithfully served it, too tenderly loved it, to bid it now farewell.   It is the Church of their fathers, the Church of their children—their first, only love.   Never will they, can they forget it.   Though separated from it by thousands of miles, they would remember it in their prayers, and help it with their money and influence.   Does the parent cast off his child who seeks a distant home? and will the child reject the parent who, by the force of circumstances, leaves him?   No, neither will these loved and trusty ones desert us.

Our history, my friends, is precious, it is worth more than our property.   The names of these dear fathers in the ministry, and of the

lamented Brodhead and McLean, are with us.
But more than all our hope is in God. He has
led us, and will lead us. The banner of his love
is floating over us. His arm defends us; his voice
cheers us. In his strength we go forward.

And now farewell, old sanctuary! Peace is
written over thy door. (*See Note G.*) May the
peace which has here ever reigned dwell in each
of our hearts, and be our watchword in all our new
relations! Farewell, ye walls which have often
echoed with the voices of those now singing in
glory! Farewell, consecrated ground, on which
our fathers built a house for God! Farewell, old
scenes, in which for many happy years we have
commingled! Farewell, dear friends, from whom
we part! Beloved hearers, may we all sit together
in heavenly places in Christ Jesus, *here* if we
may—but whether here or not, at last and forever
in that temple not made with hands, eternal in
the heaven!

And now unto Him that is able to do exceeding abundantly above all that we ask or think, according to the power that worketh in us: unto Him be glory in the Church by Christ Jesus, throughout all ages, world without end.   Amen!

NOTES.

NOTE A, Page 17.

THE Consistory, feeling greatly indebted to their beloved Treasurer for his long and efficient services, through a committee signified their intention to present him with a set of silver plate as a mark of their love for him, and appreciation of his efforts for the prosperity of their Zion. This he declined receiving on the ground of its expense. Accordingly, a large and handsome gold medal was procured from Ball, Black & Co., which was presented to Mr. Kip, on Thursday evening, May 10th, 1860, the Consistory being present, and the Pastor making the presentation address. The following are the inscriptions:

Elected Treasurer, Feb. 21, 1824.
Resigned, April 13 1833.
Reelected, May 14, 1838.
Resigned, May 1, 1860.

TO
Leonard W. Rip. Esq.
from the Consistory of the
Reformed Dutch Church
in Broome Street, N.Y.
in remembrance of services
rendered as Treasurer for
upwards of 33 years.

NOTE B, PAGE 18.

The remains of Mrs. Mc Lean were removed a few days subsequent to the final services in the church. They were found in an undisturbed state. So peacefully had they reposed for thirty-five years in their resting-place, that when the coffin was opened, the features of the countenance were as plainly distinguishable as in life. This sacred dust is now lying in a private vault in the cemetery of the Reformed Dutch Church in Houston street.

NOTE C, PAGE 24.

In liquidating this and other debts, incurred in our early history, two gentlemen of means and influence took a prominent part, and to them is to be attributed much of our past prosperity. The name of one has been mentioned. It is but justice to record the name of the other, Hon. *Myn-*

dert Van Schaick, who was not only a staunch friend in the olden time, but since his removal has ever evinced as well as expressed his regard for our continued welfare.

NOTE D, PAGE 46.

The debt in 1857 amounted to $15,000. The financial crisis which soon after visited this community, and which more or less affected all our metropolitan Churches, increased it to $17,000. This amount was accordingly taken up, and a Church bond given for its future payment, and the floating obligations were canceled. The following year a floating debt was added of $1,000, and this, despite all efforts to prevent it. Early in 1859 the Consistory foresaw they would need at least $2,000 to carry them through the ensuing year, and applied to the gentleman who held the bond of $17,000 to add to it that amount. This he declined doing. Other parties refused to loan the amount on account of the preceding bond. The only alternative was for the Consistory to put their note in the bank, endorsed by them individually. This note was to mature in May, 1860, and the only way to meet it, and also to escape the tide of the future rolling in still more heavily, was to sell the property. The congregation had repeatedly been consulted in this matter. They had been asked to come to the rescue. They could not. The inevitable necessity, therefore, was to sell or be sold.

NOTE E, PAGE 49.

The Rev. Mr. Van Nest and Dr. Bethune, associated in the pastorate of the Reformed Dutch Church in Twenty-first street, deploring the removal of the Broome Street Church, very kindly expressed a willingness to take charge of the field. Great hopes were at one time cherished by the Pastor and Consistory that some arrangement might be made. They were prepared to make sacrifices for its accomplishment. But in a conversation which these gentlemen held with our Treasurer, and also in a note addressed by one of them to the Pastor, they finally expressed themselves as compelled to decline moving in the matter.

NOTE F, Page 54.

When the present pastor came in charge of this Church, he was quite curious to learn who was the generous "lady of the Broome Street Reformed Dutch Church," whose contribution of one hundred dollars every quarter of a year to the General Synod's Board of Domestic Missions, was acknowledged in the *Christian Intelligencer*. To his surprise he found she had moved to Philadelphia and joined a Presbyterian Church in that city. But her heart was still in the Broome Street Church, with which she had been connected nearly thirty years. The sum of four hundred dollars annually she gave to support the Rev. Jerome A. Davenport as an itinerant missionary in the west. This she continued to give until last year, when Mr. Davenport, on account of his health, took a permanent charge, and the itinerant mission became vacant. I do not feel at liberty to name one who has unostentatiously styled herself "the Lady of the Broome Street Reformed Dutch Church." I doubt not her name is written in the Lamb's book of life. May she realize the promise "*His leaf also shall not wither, and whatsoever he doeth shall prosper!*"

4

NOTE G, Page 65.

INSCRIPTION ON THE CHURCH DOOR.

REFORMED

PROTESTANT DUTCH CHURCH.

ERECTED, A. D., 1823.

Peace be within thy Walls.
Psa. cxxii : 7.

SEAL OF THE CHURCH.

PASTORS.

Rev. Robert Mc Lean,   from 1824 to 1826

Rev. Jacob Brodhead, D.D.,   " 1826 " 1837

Rev. Sam'l A. Van Vranken, D.D., " 1837 " 1841

Rev. George H. Fisher, D.D.,   " 1841 " 1854

Rev. Henry V. Voorhees,   " 1855 " 1855

Rev. Peter Stryker,   " 1856 " —

TREASURERS.

Leonard W. Kip, Esq.,   from 1823 to 1835

William Hardenbrook, Jr.,   " 1835 " 1838

Leonard W. Kip, Esq.   " 1838 " 1860

CLERKS.

James Smith,	from 1823 to 1826
Anthony Woodward,	" 1826 " 1831
David M. Moore,	" 1831 " 1833
Bauman Lowe,	" 1833 " 1840
Eder V. Haughwout,	" 1840 " 1846
Henry Paterson,	" 1846 " 1847
John S. Woodward,	" 1847 " 1849
Solomon S. Kimball,	" 1849 " 1852
Oscar Schenck,	" 1852 " 1853
Henry Camerden, Jr.,	" 1853 " 1854
James V. Freeman,	" 1854 " 1857
Richard Stout, Jr.,	" 1857 " 1858
Archibald Wight,	" 1858 " 1859
Abm. C. Stryker,	" 1859 " —

ELDERS.

Luke Hinchcliff

Stephen Hasbrock, M.D.

James Ackerman

Abraham Van Cleef

Robert Buchan

John Atwood

John Ganse

William Keily

Aaron Brinckerhoff

William Poe

Joseph Martin

Anthony Woodward

Joseph Concklin

Edward Meeks

Lewis Thornell

Sylvester Earle

Caleb D. Haviland

William Woram

David Gulick

Peter Morris

Edmund Arrowsmith

William Hardenbrook, Jr.

Abraham D. Stephens

William P. Stoutenburgh

Joseph Frear

Richard Wight

Cornelius Jacobus

Bauman Lowe

Samuel Eells

John M. Ryer

Thomas Boyd, M.D.

Louis J. Belloni

Theophilus L. Houghton

John S. Woodward

William Kirby

John Woolsey

Leonard W. Kip

Benjamin Wood

George Mather

Daniel Howell

John S. Hoagland

Lawrence Wiseburn

James Dailey

Thomas Riley

Harvey Miner

Albert Slauson

John C. Barclay

Nicholas Rogers

Henry Camerden, Jr.

Hiram B. Jackson

DEACONS.

John Butler

James Smith

William Keily

John J. Ruton, M.D.

Sylvester Earle

Anthony Woodward

William Woram

Jacob Bogert

Joseph Concklin

Caleb D. Haviland

David C. Buchan

Edwin A. Dodge

Leonard W. Kip

Elnathan H. Sears

Henry V. Garretson

Henry Lippincott

Abraham Lott

David M. Moore

James Anderson, M.D.

Peter Morris

William W. Cowan

Bauman Lowe

William Fordham

Cornelius C. Jacobus

Andrew Wight

Theophilus L. Houghton

John M. Ryer

Lawrence Proudfoot, M.D.

Louis J. Belloni

Nicholas D. Herder

Eder V. Haughwout

Abraham D. Weeks

John Gray

John N. Genin

John S. Woodward

David Beach

Robert Smith

William Becker

Henry Patterson

John M. Roome

Richard Voorhis

John Williamson

Solomon S. Kimball

A. A. Mc Withey

Thomas Barry

Peter Duryee

Horatio J. Ware

John C. Barclay

Gideon Jennings

Henry Camerden, Jr.

John A. Van Buskirk

James V. Freeman

Harvey Miner

John S. Martin

Richard Stout

Thomas Little

Myron K. Moore

Archibald Wight

James W. Purdy, M.D.

John D. Watson

Abraham O. Stryker

Ira H. Tompkins

Henry C. Halsey

Samuel V. S. Mandeville

Abraham A. Stager

www.ingramcontent.com/pod-product-compliance
Lightning Source LLC
Chambersburg PA
CBHW031452270326
41930CB00007B/959